Stitching with
Beatrix Potter

Michele Hill

Author Michele Hill
michelehillquilts.com
williammorrisandmichele.blogspot.com.au

Photography Michele Hill

Additional Photo credits:

Page 7/8 - Beatrix Potter with her father and brother, Lindeth Howe
Lindeth Howe Country Hotel, lindeth-howe.co.uk

Hill Top path, Hill Top Farm, Castle Cottage, Herdwick sheep
Betsy Bray, betsybray.org

Page 52 - 1863 Rupert and Helen Potter Wedding Quilt
National Trust Hill Top, nationaltrust.org.uk/hill-top

First Published in Australia 2016
Printed by allBIZ Supplies | allbizsupplies.biz

Stitching with Beatrix Potter

Exclusive Distributor:
C&T Publishing, Inc.
P.O. Box 1456
Lafayette, CA 94549
800.284.1114
ctpub.com

ISBN 978-1-61745-610-7

Printed in China

10 9 8 7 6 5 4 3 2 1

Contents

Welcome

August of 2010 was the first time I met Helen Bertram of Whitecroft Tours in person and one of the first things she said to me was: "You have to write a Beatrix Potter book!" She had seen rabbits and ducks in my nursery quilts in my 2010 book *More William Morris in Appliqué* where I had recorded my love of growing up with Beatrix Potter books. So it has taken just six years and I have finally done it. One of the things that Helen really wanted me to avoid was a book full of "cutsie wootise" characters and focus on Beatrix Potter the artist, scientist and conservationist, so I hope I have managed to do that.

As I write this I have vivid thoughts of my recent (and very first), visit to Japan in January of 2016. I had heard that there were to be two special displays of both William Morris and Beatrix Potter inspired quilts at the 2016 Tokyo Quilt Festival. It was not something on my bucket list but when I found out there was to be both a William Morris and Beatrix Potter quilt display I just had to go! It was here that I saw the most incredible hand stitched quilts I had ever seen in over 30 years of quilting! The hand appliqué and embroidery adorning these Beatrix Potter inspired quilts were from Yoko Saito and a group of ten other quilters. Under Yoko's direction each quilter had painstakingly reproduced Beatrix's characters and stories with meticulous detail and accuracy. My immediate reaction was to phone Larry at home and tell him that my attempts at producing a Beatrix Potter quilt book seemed worthless and maybe I should bin the idea! At this stage I had actually completed all the projects and just had the typing to do. But in Larry's wise words he reminded me that perhaps what I had seen would be unachievable to many–including myself! So here is my version that I hope will appeal to all levels of stitcher, from novice to expert. The most challenging project is the 1863 Wedding quilt which should have been hand pieced to replicate the original. But with time constraints and my dislike of piecing I decided to complete it entirely by machine and all in appliqué.

While reading Linda Lear's biography of Beatrix Potter, I discovered a possible connection between Beatrix and William Morris! Beatrix sent her early stories to the grandchildren of Edward Burne-Jones, Morris's lifetime friend and business partner. I also learnt that Beatrix's father Rupert was a professional photographer and was often asked by another Pre-Raphaelite artist, Sir John Everett Millais, to photograph subjects or scenes for his paintings. Beatrix was also an active member of the Society for the Protection of Ancient Buildings that Morris formed in 1877. Like Morris, she appreciated handcrafted work and had a mutual love of nature in the Arts & Crafts style. So through these connections I wonder if William and Beatrix actually ever met?

Acknowledgements

Once again I find myself expressing my overwhelming gratitude to Helen Bertram of Whitecroft tours in the UK for planting the seed for a Beatrix Potter book all those years ago. Helen also offered to write the history for me so I didn't let her forget! I must also mention that Helen was the Chairman of the UK Beatrix Potter Society for several years and has great knowledge of her. In fact, she once told me she is as obsessed with Beatrix Potter as I am with William Morris! Thank you so much, Helen, for your knowledge and time, and I hope that this book might result in more people learning more about this wonderful author/artist–Beatrix Potter–as I did!

Special thanks also go to Helen for following up on images for me. A special thank you to Alison Magee-Barker FIH, General Manager, and Clare Bateman, Assistant Manager of Lindeth Howe Country House Hotel (*www.lindeth-howe.co.uk*), for supplying the historical images of Beatrix Potter and Lindeth Howe. Helen also introduced me to Betsy Bray (*www.betsybray.org*), who so kindly supplied photos of Hill Top Farm and the Herdwick sheep. Betsy resides in the US and has been a member of the Beatrix Potter Society since 1984. Thanks also to Liz Hunter MacFarlane from the UK National Trust and Hill Top (*www.nationaltrust.org.uk/hill-top*), for sending me the image of the 1863 wedding quilt. I feel extremely blessed and honoured that I was given permission to reproduce this historical "Potter" quilt for the book.

Thank you to everyone that I've met on my quilting journey and especially for being so supportive of my first self-published book *Afternoon Tea with May Morris*–that was the trial run before taking on this challenge!

I must also mention Pamela, who I met at a quilt show in Bordertown. I was a guest at the show where I was hand stitching the Hill Top wool felt box. I was wondering what I should add and a few weeks later after meeting Pamela, a delightful letter came in the post with a sample suggesting a trailing vine and leaves–well, I had already started on the wisteria, but Pamela, I wanted to thank you anyway! I give thanks every day for my special quilting friends that I meet with regularly. You always encourage me and for that I am so grateful.

My thanks again to Di and Wink from Allbiz Supplies, South Australia, for again providing their expertise-and especially the kind and patient Wink! He is always so helpful and full of so many ideas with layout. You're the best, Wink!

And as always I am forever grateful to my daughters and their partners for the time this all takes, and of course I could not do this without my best friend and husband. His unwavering support is truly incredible and if it wasn't for him this book would not even be a consideration. Thank you, Larry, from the bottom of my heart.

Beatrix Potter's writing desk at Hilltop

Beatrix Potter 1866-1943

Helen Beatrix Potter was born at Bolton Gardens, London on 28th July 1866, the first child of Helen and Rupert Potter. Beatrix wrote, aged 75, that even though she and her brother, Bertram, were born in London–"*our interests and our joy were in the North Country.*"

Hill Top path

Like many wealthy Victorian children, she did not see her parents very often but was looked after by a nurse and educated at home by a governess. Beatrix did not have many friends her own age because her parents did not want her to pick up bad habits or illness, but she had her younger brother, Bertram, for company and they were allowed to keep a great variety of pets–rabbits, mice, lizards, a snake, a bat, a frog and a tortoise. The children studied these animals carefully, recording their habits and making sketches of them.

As Beatrix grew older her father began to take her to art exhibitions and she met several influential artists, including John Millais. Around this time, at the age of 15, she began to keep a diary written in secret code. She wrote about people she met and the exhibitions she visited. This code was not cracked until several years after her death.

For the first fifteen years of her life the family spent their holidays in Scotland and it was here that she met Charles McIntosh, a revered naturalist and mycologist who helped her with the accuracy of her illustrations. In her sixteenth year her father chose a new place for their annual holiday- Wray Castle in the Lake District. Beatrix was enamoured of this area and longed to return one day to live. One of the regular visitors to their holiday home was Canon Rawnsley, an intelligent and articulate man in his thirties. He and Beatrix became good friends and they discussed geology and archaeology and he introduced her to his ideas on conservation. Canon Rawnsley was a keen campaigner for local environmental issues. He protested against the extension of the railway line into the Lake District, as well as the closure of ancient footpaths. Beatrix never forgot these concerns and she also became an environmental campaigner, long before the cause became fashionable. She successfully fought plans to build an aeroplane factory in the Lakes and drew up a petition. The land and farms that she eventually bought from the proceeds of her "little books" were given to the National Trust.

In the 1890s her mycological illustrations and research into the reproduction of fungus spores generated interest from the scientific establishment. She produced a paper which was submitted to the Linnean Society, but due to her gender and amateur status, it was rejected. In 1997 the Linnean Society issued a posthumous apology to Potter.

When Bertram was eleven he was sent away to boarding school and Beatrix remained at home and had a new governess, Annie Carter. They were of a similar age and became close friends. When Annie left to marry Edwin Moore, Beatrix kept in touch and when Annie's son Noel was ill, she wrote a picture letter to him, telling the story of a naughty rabbit called Peter and his adventures in Mr McGregor's garden. This became one of the most famous letters ever written and was the basis of the first of 23 little books eventually published. It never occurred to her to turn her stories into books but with the support and encouragement of Canon Rawnsley, she submitted it to eight publishers–all of whom rejected it. She was so determined to see her book in print that she published it herself and sold it to her friends and family. It was so successful that a year later the family firm of Frederick Warne agreed to publish it. This was *The Tale of Peter Rabbit* and the year was 1902.

With the money she made from these books she was able to buy Hill Top Farm in Near Sawrey in the Lake District. She employed John Cannon to run the farm for her and she

Beatrix with her father Rupert and brother Bertram

visited as often as she could. Whilst at Hill Top she continued to write her little books and many of the illustrations can be seen in and around the village.

Hill Top farm

During her dealings with the publishers at Frederick Warne, Beatrix became very close to Norman Warne, the youngest son. In 1905 Norman proposed marriage but her parents strongly disapproved as he "was in trade." Sadly, a few weeks later, Norman was taken ill and died. Beatrix was heartbroken. In order to recover from her grief, Beatrix threw herself into work. She also began to buy more land and property in the Lake District and employed a local solicitor, William Heelis, to help her buy land and advise her of any new property coming to the market. In 1912, when she was almost 47 years old, William Heelis proposed marriage to her. Again her parents disapproved but Beatrix was determined that they would not interfere with her happiness and on the 15th of October 1913, she became Mrs. William Heelis.

After her marriage, Beatrix dedicated her life almost entirely to farming and particularly to breeding Herdwick Sheep. She employed a local farmer, Tom Storey, to take care of her flocks.

Castle Cottage at Castle Farm where Beatrix died. She lived there for 30 years with William Heelis.

She became a well respected judge at agricultural shows and became the first woman to be elected President of the Herdwick Sheepbreeders' Association. In her old age Beatrix could be seen tramping around the Lake District wearing a pair of old clogs, an apron and tweeds made from Herdwick wool.

Herdwick sheep

After the death of her Father Rupert, in 1914, Beatrix bought Lindeth Howe for her mother–this became her home and was only a short distance across Lake Windermere. A dutiful daughter, Beatrix could be seen walking down the lanes around Sawrey and taking the ferry across the Lake to her Mother's home. In 1923 she acquired Troutbeck Farm and in 1930 she bought the large Monk Coniston estate, saving it from the developers. Over the next few years she acquired several other farms and cottages. By the time she died in 1943, at the age of 77, she had become a well respected member of the hill farming community, and on her death she left 1600 hectares (4,000 acres) of land to the National Trust, including 15 farms and many cottages. She is credited with preserving much of the land that now comprises the Lake District National Park.

Lindeth Howe

Helen Bertram
December 2015

General Instructions

These instructions are *common to most projects*. When you see **"Refer to General Instructions"** refer back here.

Appliqué Tips:

Vliesofix is still my preferred **fusible appliqué paper** for raw edge appliqué. I do prefer the 45 cm wide roll and always store it on a cardboard roll in a dry dark cupboard. Never put a rubber band around the roll. The friction of moving the band on and off may contribute to that pesky issue of the web coming away from the paper!

My favourite **scissors** for cutting my appliqué pieces are Fiskars *Softgrip*. They have a fine sharp point and large handles for comfort.

(www3.fiskars.com)

An **open-toed appliqué foot** is a must on your machine for appliqué. The wide open foot gives a clear view of sharp points. Take the stitch one step at a time and work around the points slowly counting the steps as you go.

Generally you never turn your work unless the needle is outside your appliqué. Also, engage the *needle down* position if available on your machine.

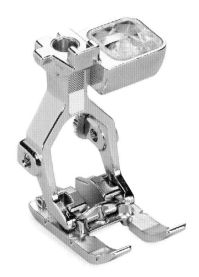

Open-toed foot (www.bernina.com)

More recently my preferred needle is a *Topstitch* No. 70/10 made by the Superior company. I also like to put my threads on a thread stand also made by Superior.

(www.superiorthreads.com)

Machine appliqué technique:

Stabilising the back of your work before stitching the appliqué is a personal choice. I do not do it unless I am using a dense blanket stitch like satin stitch. Appliqué around each shape using desired stitch (blanket, zigzag etc.). This can be done by hand or machine.

1. Trace all the appliqué shapes from the pattern sheet onto the paper side (smooth side) of the fusible web, leaving at least ½″ between each shape. Take note of the dotted lines where some pieces will need to go under other sections. Also note that images *have already been reversed* for your convenience as this is required for this method. Do not spread designs too far apart, making economical use of fabric. Work with one pattern and one colour of fabric at a time.

2. Roughly cut around each shape (not on the traced line at this stage) and using a hot dry iron, apply each shape to the wrong side of your chosen fabric. When the shapes are ironed on, cut them out again, this time on the traced line.

3. Now you are ready to remove the backing paper and press pieces in place.

4. If you have a light box this can assist with placement. Place pattern page wrong side down on your light box (because pattern has already been reversed) and place background fabric on top of pattern page. Take note of any sections that tuck under some pieces.

5. Sometimes it is helpful to assemble pieces on an appliqué mat (or baking paper) where you are able to assemble the entire piece in one. With all sections ready and still using the lightbox and reversed pattern page, place pieces on to the appliqué mat, press and wait until it is cool. You can now peel off the entire design in one. See photos of the Mrs Tiggy Winkle project done in this way. I also find tweezers are very useful for placing pieces under other pieces–fingers can be very clumsy!

TIP! When tracing appliqué designs ensure you trace either directly on the line or just inside it. The design may end up too large if you trace outside the line. Also be aware that if photocopying the design, some photocopiers can cause a slight change in size.

Appliqué - Machine technique:

I like to use a small machine blanket stitch on my appliqué. Be careful not to go too narrow into the appliqué as the appliqué may lift over time. On my Bernina 570QE I usually set my width and length to 1.7 but every machine is a little different.

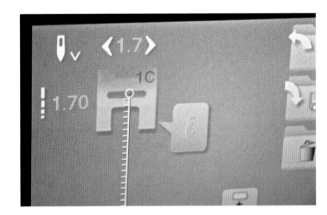

If the sewing machine does not have a blanket stitch, try adjusting the width and length of the blind hem stitch (if possible) to achieve a mock blanket stitch.

To improve stitch accuracy with an uninterrupted view of the edge of the appliqué shape, work the machine stitching using an open-toed appliqué/embroidery presser foot on your sewing machine. Place the machine embroidery thread in the top of the machine with a neutral or matching coloured thread on the bobbin.

Always check your tensions whenever you change threads as different weights need different adjustments. If the bobbin thread is showing on the top of your appliqué turn the tension to a lower number. Top tension can be adjusted manually. Follow your machine manual instructions. So if 4 is normal you may have to turn tension down to 3 or even 2. Sometimes you may need to adjust your bobbin tension. Check this by lifting out your bobbin shuttle. Hold the thread above the shuttle and gently jerk it. If the thread shuttle falls away quickly it means the tension is too loose. Turn the screw very slightly to the right to tighten ("righty tighty"). If the shuttle doesn't shift at all it is too tight so you need to turn the screw slightly to the left to loosen ("lefty loosey").

If your machine has a tie off, stitch test this first to ensure it does not unravel. Alternatively, there are a number of other ways you can tie off your work at the beginning and end:

- pull threads to the back of your work and tieoff by hand

- do a couple of straight stitches before commencing blanket stitch

- turn the width of the blanket stitch to zero, then stitch a couple of stitches before turning the width up again

Threads: To get a delicate fine blanket stitch I usually use machine embroidery thread on the top and a neutral similar weight thread in the bobbin. Friends had been telling me about the joy of using Aurifil threads and I am now a convert.

TIP! Clean your machine with a brush, and oil as directed in your manual—and do change the needles regularly!

I found the orange spools Mako' NE 50/2 beautiful to use. I used the black shade of this thread in the top and bobbin for my entire appliqué in both the Bubbles Nursery Quilt and the 1863 wedding quilt. For other projects I used machine embroidery threads, my favourites being the Maderia brand, Wonderfil's Splendor range and Magnifico from Superior threads.

Bindings:

When I first started making quilts it seemed to be standard to cut binding strips 2½″ wide but over time I found that some of my quilt edges were not tight and firm as they should be. One of the key areas that is looked for with judging and valuing quilts is the binding and I understand they must be "fat and full"!

So then I started cutting my bindings 2¼″ wide but it was oh-so-hard pulling it to the back to hand stitch. So now I have gone back to 2½″ wide strips but when I attach them to my quilt I use a ⅝″ seam allowance–a little wider than ¼″. I also attach my bindings to the quilt top before the excess backing and batting is trimmed away. I like that extra bit to hold on to as I attach the binding.

I join all strips with a 45-degree angle and press the seams open.

1. Using a ¼″ seam, attach the binding starting in the centre of one side (I prefer to start on the base). Make sure you have about 6″ to play with at the beginning and end of your binding strips.

2. Stop ¼″ from each corner and secure with a backstitch.

3. Turn work so stitching is horizontal at the top. Fold binding up and then down to create a 45 degree fold.

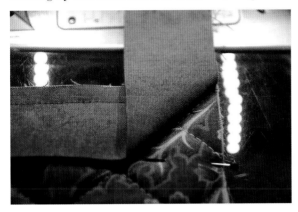

4. Pin in place and continue with ¼″ seam.

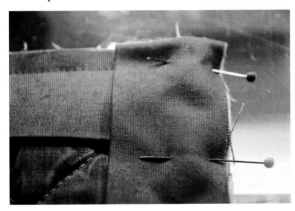

When I get to the end of the quilt I also join the strips on a 45-degree angle and many years ago I found an amazing formula. This is a brief summary of how to do that:

1. Finish attaching the binding strip to the quilt top about 6″ from where you started.

2. Fold back both the beginning and the end strip along the edge of the quilt so that the folded edges butt together. Make sure the binding lays flat against the quilt and then finger press the fold where they meet.

3. Trim a little less than half the measurement of your cut binding strips. So if your strips were cut 2½″ trim back from fold a little less than 1¼″ as seen in photo. Cut the second side at 2½″.

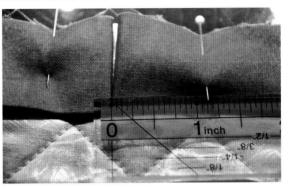

4. Open both strips and place the ends on a 45 degree angle as you would if you were joining the strips. The bulk of your quilt or cushion top should be against your body with the raw edge away from you. Pin and stitch along the 45-degree angle and then trim to ¼″.

5. Finger press the seam open, fold wrong side of binding strips together and then pin to the quilt or cushion edge. The measurement will be perfect and you can complete the last step of attaching your binding and no one will know where you started or ended!

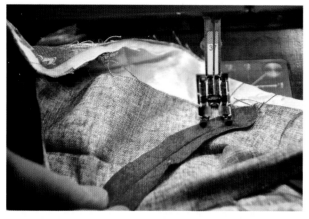

Hand Embroidery stitches:

I am not an expert embroiderer and only know the basics. There are lots of resources online that can help you. My favourite is Mary Corbet's site, *www.needlenthread.com*, where you will find stitches galore. And of course a resource book is a must and my absolute favourite and I think one of the best is Yvette Stanton's book, *The Right Handed Embroiderer's Companion–a Step by Step Stitch Dictionary*. It is also available for left-handers as well (as Yvette is and why the book came about), and is available online and in stores.

Note: my images were stitched with a thick thread and a large needle to assist visually.

Back Stitch:

1. Bring the needle from under your work and proceed with a running stitch. Bring needle up and back down into the end of the previous stitch.

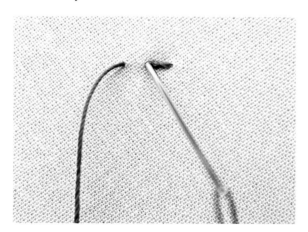

2. Continue in this manner.

Chain Stitch:

1. Bring the needle from under your work and proceed with a running stitch but looping the thread under the needle as you move forward.

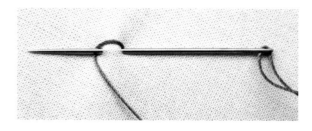

2. Pull thread gently forward as you take out your needle. Insert needle back into the chain that has formed and repeat step 1.

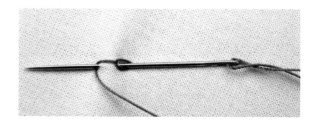

French Knot:

1. Bring the needle from under your work and wrap thread around needle twice.

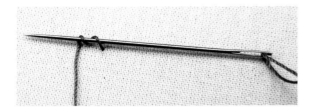

2. With gentle tension on the thread (so that wraps do not unravel), take your needle back into a hole beside the previous one and pull through gently to make a French knot. Do not pull too tight or the knot will disappear to the underside of your work.

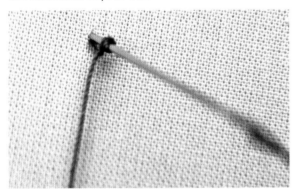

Satin Stitch:

1. Always start in the centre of your design.

2. Bring needle from under work and stitch a straight stitch over to opposite side of design.

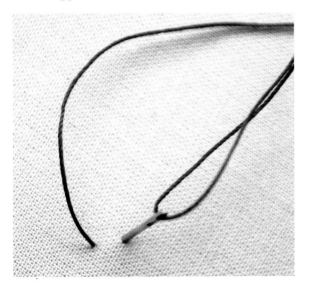

3. Take needle from underneath and return to the start–just beside the beginning of the first stitch.

4. Repeat to the length of desired design.

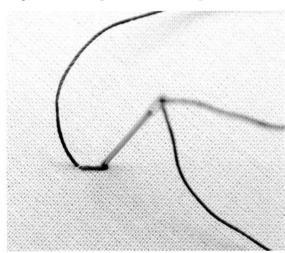

5. Once the top half of the design is complete return to the start and work your way down the other side.

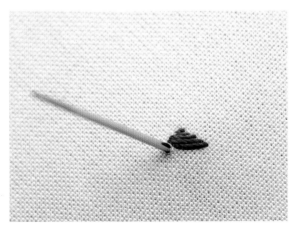

Whip Stitch:

1. The first step to this stitch commences underneath the appliqué and goes out to the background. Take needle out to background edge and come back out under appliqué but long the length slightly.

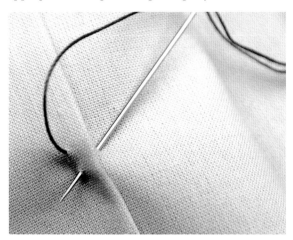

2. Gently pull stitch closed and move forward and repeat step 2.

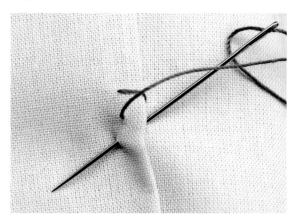

3. As you can see in the photo it is really just a stitch that goes over and over the raw edge–ideal for wool felt.

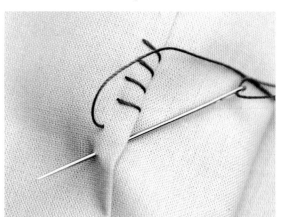

Stem Stitch:

1. Begin by bringing work up from underneath. Working left to right in photo (you can work the opposite way), take a backstitch pointing back to the beginning. Make sure your thread is below the needle.

2. Repeat step 1 taking the needle out at then end of the very first stitch.

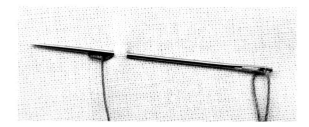

3. Continue this way ensuring your thread is always below the needle.

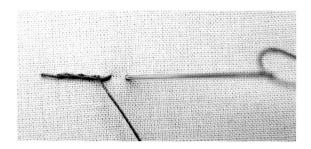

"P" is for Pinwheels

I am absolutely obsessed with pinwheels so I just had to do one for the book! In my *Afternoon Tea with May Morris* book I designed some larger ones to become coasters, but these are small as they would have traditionally been in the 19th century and earlier. I have used a recycled vintage doily that I purchased at a charity shop to cover my pinwheels. The doily was unfinished and was slightly stained but was perfect for cutting up and then embellishing with some little Beatrix Potter characters. You can make any size you like from two to four inch circles or larger. My instructions are for a four-inch pinwheel using cardboard drink coasters that I purchased from Ikea.

You will need:

For each **pinwheel**:

- Background fabric (cream doily)
  15 cm × 30 cm (6″ × 12″)
- Small scraps of contrast for appliqué (duck, rabbit and wren pattern included)
- Matching threads for appliqué (Stranded cottons for hand appliqué or machine embroidery threads for machine)
- Perle cotton in contrasting colour to join circles

- Beads or pins to decorate edge
- Fusible appliqué paper
- Two 10 cm (4″) circles of template plastic or cardboard coasters of the same size (Ikea!)
- Two 10 cm (4″) circles of batting
- Two 9.5 cm (3¾″) circles of batting

Method:

1. From the background fabric (or doily), cut two 6″ circles and mark an X in the centre of one.

2. Following the **General Instructions** (page 9) and taking note of the centre X appliqué each circle with a motif of choice.

3. When appliqué is complete gather outer edge with a double strand of sewing thread. Before gathering, place the 4″ circle of batting inside the wrong side, followed by the 3¾″ batting circle and then finally the 4″ circle of template plastic (or cardboard drink coaster).

4. Repeat for the other side.

5. Join the two covered discs together by using a *glove stitch* with perle cotton and your choice of colour.

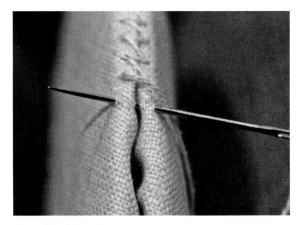

Glove Stitch Step 1

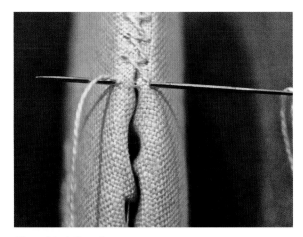

Glove Stitch Step 2

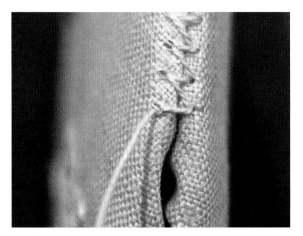

Glove Stitch Step 3

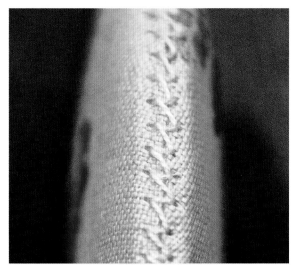

Glove Stitch completed

6. Finally add pins or beads of choice to decorate edge.

Mrs Tiggy-Winkle Iron Cover

My iron lives on a shelf in the laundry and I often think it could do with a dust cover–so Mrs Tiggy-Winkle seemed like the perfect project! I would love Mrs Tiggy-Winkle in my home–she was most particular about washing, starching and above all, ironing clothes: *"And she gave them their nice clean clothes; and all the little animals and birds were so very much obliged to dear Mrs. Tiggy-Winkle."* I constructed my cover with three triangular sections using a pre-quilted calico for the outer covering and quilter's muslin for the lining.

These instructions were for my Tefal iron that measures 12″ high and 6″ wide at the base. Adust to fit your iron by tracing around the triangular shape of the sole-plate, tapering sides to fit, and adding 2″ to this tracing (this gives a 1″ seam allowance which can be trimmed back after basting if it seems too big).

You will need:

- Outer fabric (or pre-quilted calico) 50 cm × 110 cm (20″ × 43″)
- Lining fabric (quilter's muslin) 50 cm × 110 cm (20″ × 43″)
- Small pieces for appliqué (see photo for detail)
- Matching background thread for cover construction
- Matching threads for appliqué (Stranded cottons for hand appliqué or machine embroidery threads for machine)

- 30 cm × 30 cm (12″ × 12″) piece of fusible appliqué paper
- 50 cm × 110 cm (20″ × 43″) piece of batting (I used a thermal batting with insulation properties)
- 2 metres (2⅛ yard) × 5 cm (2″) wide bias binding (I used a pre-purchased black and white striped binding. You could make your own and there are lots of sites on the internet to help you. I found this video and step by step instructions link excellent on McCall's Quilting site: *mccallsquilting.com > lessons > continuous bias*)

Method:

1. From the outer fabric cut three triangular shapes from the pattern (pullout page P1). Seam allowance has been included but adjust to fit your own iron as required. Repeat for lining fabric.

2. Appliqué the design to one outer shape taking note of the position on the background as indicated on the pattern page (base of Mrs Tiggy-Winkle's foot is 2½″ from raw edge).

3. Following the **General Instructions** (page 9) complete the appliqué.

4. Cut three triangular shapes from the thermal batting.

5. Place pieces in the following order: lining right side down, batting then appliqué right side up. Pin baste and then stitch around all three layers close to the edge. Repeat for the other three sections.

6. Following the photo instructions pin two basted cover sections together and then pin the binding to the curved section. Using a ½″ seam allowance attach the binding taking note of the tight curve at the top section.

7. Turn binding to other side and using a blind hemstitch hand stitch in place. Trim.

8. Join the third basted cover section to the two sides that have no binding. Repeat as before taking note of the raw edge of the previous binding that needs tucking inside.

9. Finally attach binding to the base of the iron cover.

Bubbles Nursery Quilt and Bunting

Beatrix Potter is of course synonymous with her tales of Peter Rabbit and his many friends. So there just had to be a quilt for little people featuring some of her characters like Jemima Puddle-duck, Mr Todd the fox, Mr Jeremy Fisher the frog and Mr Brown the owl. Mrs Tittlemouse the wood mouse could not stand untidiness: *"Never did I see such a mess-smears of honey; and moss, and thistledown-and marks of big and little dirty feet-all over my nice clean house!"* So Mrs Tittlemouse also adorns the quilt with her cleaning rag in hand!

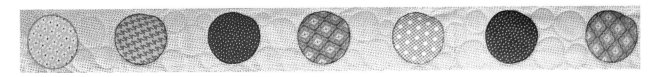

You will need:

- Background fabric for inner blocks, sashings and outer border fabric 1.3 metres (1½ yards) x width of fabric (110 cm) (51″ × 43″)

- Assorted bright feature prints—a total of nine different strips x 2½″ wide are required for the strips around each block (One strip x width for each block. I had a jelly roll which was perfect for this. If you use the same print around each block you will need 60–70 cm or 24″–28″ in total)

- Binding 40 cm (15¾″) x width of fabric (110 cm or 43″)

- Backing fabric needs to measure 125 cm × 140 cm (49″ × 55″)

- Batting needs to measure 125 cm × 140 cm (49″ × 55″)

- An assortment of co-ordinating fabrics for the appliqué in each block and for the circles (In total I appliquéd 24 x 9 cm (3½″) circles and 34 x 5 cm (2″) circles in the sashings and outer border. The jelly roll was again useful for the 2″ circles)

- Black thread for appliqué (I appliquéd the entire quilt in black and I am pleased with the definition it has given to the appliqué)

- Grey or beige thread (a neutral colour) for piecing and matching background thread to quilt

- Fusible appliqué paper

- Piece of template plastic to make a 5 cm (2″) circle and a 9 cm (3½″) circle

Cutting:

1. From the background fabric cut two 8½″ strips across the width of fabric and then crosscut to yield nine 6½″ × 8½″ rectangles. These will be your nine background blocks ready for appliqué. You will have some fabric left from the 8½″ strips for orphan blocks or back up for mistakes. I used a block to make a bag–see photo at end of project.

2. From background fabric cut two further strips 3″ wide and then crosscut six x 12½″ to yield six vertical sashing strips. Cut a further two 3″ × 35½″ strips for horizontal sashings. Set aside for later.

3. From the bright feature fabric surrounding each block you will need one 2½″ strip x width of fabric for each block. (I used fabrics from a jelly roll.) For each block cut two strips 2½″ × 8½″ (longer vertical sides are added first) and two further strips 2½″ × 10½″ for the top and bottom of each block.

4. Final outer borders require five strips cut 5″ wide x width of fabric. Set aside four of these strips. From the one spare strip cut two lengths x 10″ long and attach to two of the four remaining 5″ strips set aside. The two side vertical borders will need to measure 41½″ in length and the horizontal top and bottom borders need to measure 44½″ in length.

5. From the binding fabric cut six strips x 2½″ across the width.

Method:

1. Fold each of the nine blocks in half lengthways and widthways and finger press to assist with placement of appliqué. Following the **General Instructions** (page 9) appliqué all pattern pieces to the centre.

2. Using a ¼″ seam allowance and with right sides together stitch the 2½″ bright feature fabric strips to each block. Attach the long vertical sides first using the two 2½″ × 8½″ strips and then finally the two horizontal 2½″ × 10½″ strips to the top and the bottom of each block. Press seams away from the centre as you go. Blocks should now measure 10½″ × 12½″.

3. Join the blocks to the 3″ sashing strips as shown in the diagram below. One 3″ × 12½″ sashing strip is stitched to the right side of block one, block four and block seven. Then attach block two to block one, block five to block four and block eight to block seven. Repeat for remaining blocks.

4. Attach the two horizontal sashing strips between each row and press.

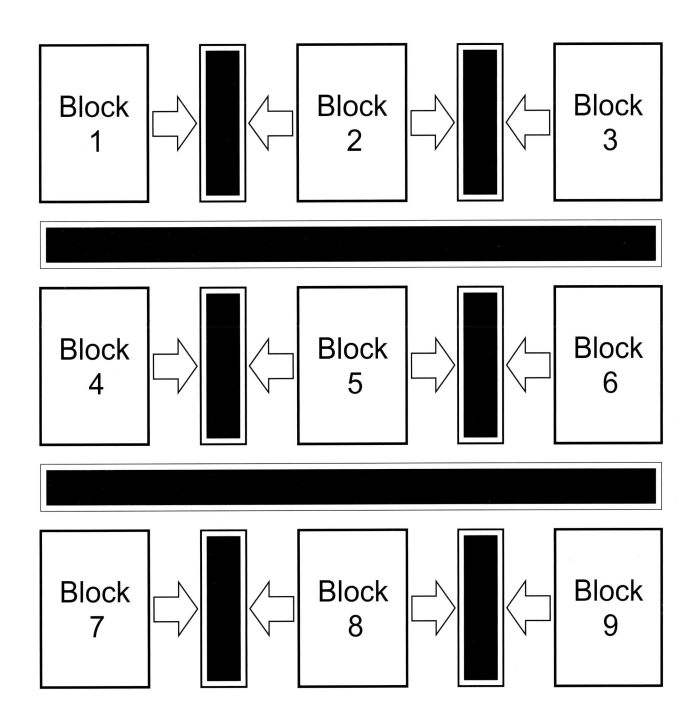

5. The final construction of the quilt is to attach the 5″ borders. Attach the vertical side borders first but check the measurement by measuring through the centre of the quilt first (sides should measure 41½″). Stitch each vertical side border and again press seam away from centre. Finally attach the horizontal borders to the top and bottom of quilt but measure through the centre of the quilt widthways to check size (which should measure 44½″).

6. Appliqué 2″ and 3½″ circles as desired following photo for placement. There are 34 x 2″ circles in the narrow sashings and 24 x 3½″ circles in the borders.

7. When all appliqué is complete, prepare backing fabric to measure approximately 49″ × 55″.

8. Sandwich the batting between the backing and the quilt top ensuring the right sides are facing outwards. Baste as desired–either pin or tack. Using a straight stitch walking foot (or engage dual feed on machine), and using matching background thread, stitch in the ditch around each block and outer sashing. Using the same thread free motion, quilt around the outside edge of the entire appliqué. To do this you need to drop your feed-dogs on the machine and then use a free-motion quilting foot. I then quilted 2″ free motion circles in the sashings and

then assorted 1–2″ size circles to fit in the borders. To assist with this step and using a non permanent marker, trace assorted circles in random sections of the borders.

9. Following the Binding section of the **General Instructions** (page 9) join on the cross, the 6 x 2½″ binding strips to make one long length. Press the strip in half, wrong sides together and raw edges even. Attach to the front of the quilt using a ¼″ seam and mitering the corners as you come to them. Trim back any excess backing and batting and fold binding to the back of the quilt and hand stitch in place.

10. Finally add a label to the back of your quilt for future generations.

Bunting:

For the bunting hanging on the wall behind the quilt I cut rectangles 8½″ × 12½″ for each "flag." Mark the rectangle as indicated below and then trim off the sides to create the bunting flag. You will need two pieces for each flag (back and front). Appliqué as desired before stitching right sides together, leaving an opening to turn right side out. Finally, attach to a ribbon or binding as desired.

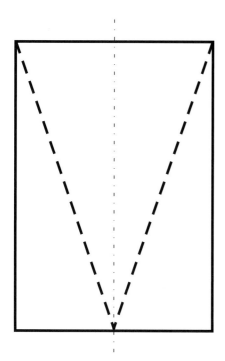

Bag:

Use your favourite method to create a bag like the library bag I've created for a little person. My bag uses the same size block as the quilt and I've attached 3½″ strips each side to create a finished bag measuring 16″ wide × 18″ long.

Let's Play - Wool Felt Baby Ball

I can recall my younger brother being given one of these wool felt balls back when he was born in the 1960s. I have no idea what happened to it but I can recall it was made of wedge shapes and different colours. This is my version with felt appliqué added. I've included a mushroom to acknowledge Beatrix Potter's incredible artwork and contribution to the discovery of a rare fungus in 1893. Beatrix Potter's fungi artwork is extraordinary and became and still is a scientific Mycology resource. It was also on this day in 1893 that Beatrix sat down and wrote a get well picture letter to five year old Noel about *"four little rabbits named Flopsy, Mopsy, Cottontail and Peter."*

You will need:

- Assorted wool felt pieces—six in total with each piece measuring 20 cm × 10 cm (8″ × 4″)
- Assorted small wool felt for appliqué
- Freezer paper—30 cm × 30 cm (12″ × 12″) should suffice
- Threads of choice to appliqué and join ball
- Chenille needle No 22
- Polyester fibrefill (just under 100 g)

NOTE:
It is important to only use wool felt and not acrylic. Wool does not stretch like acrylic. I also like to pre-wash it in a hot wash by machine as well, to strengthen and "felt" the fibres even more. You will get some shrinkage but I think it is worth it.

Method:

1. Cut six ball wedges of wool felt from the pattern (pullout page P1) in colours of your choice.

2. Trace appliqué shapes from pattern sheet on to the paper side of the freezer paper. Cut out shape and iron the shiny side to the small pieces of wool felt for appliqué. Cut around the paper template. You can re-use the freezer paper a few times but peel off gently. You may prefer to pin the templates with tiny pins and cut around the edge.

3. Appliqué shapes to each ball wedge with either a blanket stitch or a whip stitch. I find whip stitch is faster and just as secure. See **General Instructions** (page 9) for stitch directions.

4. When the appliqué is complete the wedges need to be joined one by one using a glove stitch. See step by step photos in the **Pinwheel project** (page 17) for glove stitch.

5. You will find the top of the ball needs to be left a little open so it sits flat for the final small appliquéd circle. This can be overstitched at the end.

6. Stuff the ball with the fibrefill. Leave half of the final wedge seam open for stuffing.

7. Close the top and base by appliquéing a 1¼″ felt circle in blanket stitch. I use a stitch that is sometimes called Hedebo buttonhole stitch that you can see in the photo below.

Hedebo Buttonhole stitch:

1. Bring needle from the outer edge in under the appliqué.

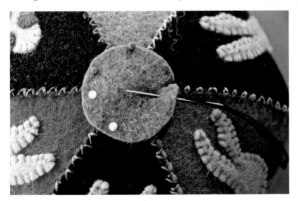

2. Pull needle gently and just before you secure the stitch tuck the needle under the loop and pull gently.

3. Pull thread gently away from the appliqué and repeat. I find this stitch very secure and it doesn't roll on the edge like a blanket stitch sometimes can.

Handmade Hexies

My collection of William Morris prints is always a pleasure to use, so with this project William Morris finally meets Beatrix Potter! I've admired quilt-as-you go hexagon quilts for several years so decided to have a go at making one myself while using my designs as stitcheries instead of appliqué. My instructions for the "quilt as you go hexagon" method are what worked for me, but if you know a different or better way please go for it! Be aware that some of the designs in the Bubbles nursery quilt may be a little large for the inside of the 8″ hexagon. If I'd had more time I would have made a much larger quilt but there is always room for that–I just need to remove the four half hexagons and then keep going. This is a fun, portable project as it is entirely stitched by hand.

You will need:

- An assortment of prints for the hexagon fronts–each one requires a 21 cm (8½″) square for the 8½″ hexagon (My quilt has 23 hexagons and 4 half hexagons)

- 50 cm (⅝ yard) of a good quality quilter's muslin for the six embroidered hexagons

- An assortment of prints for the 23 hexagon backs and four half hexagons–each one requires a 27 cm (10½″) square for the 10½″ hexagon

- Batting/wadding for hexagon centres–in total you will need 23 x 21 cm (8½″) squares–140 cm × 90 cm wide pellon (55″ × 36″) and four extra for the half hexagons

- An assortment of stranded cottons for embroidery (I used several variegated shades from Cottage Garden threads: *cottagegardenthreads.typepad.com*)

- Crewel needles, size 10 for embroidery

- Perle cotton or 12wt cotton for quilting if desired

- One 21 cm (8½″) and one 27 cm (10½″) hexagon template or template plastic to make own from template on pattern (pullout page P2)

Method:

1. If you have purchased hexagon templates you will be able to cut them from fabric with a rotary cutter. You will need 6 x 8½″ hexagon fronts of quilter's muslin and 17 x 8½″ hexagon fronts from the prints.

2. Repeat for the 23 x 10½″ hexagon backs from the prints.

3. If making templates from template plastic trace from pattern (pullout page P2) onto template plastic and cut carefully on traced line. Use this template to trace the hexagons on the same number of required shapes on the wrong side of the fabric. Cut hexagon shapes with scissors or follow traced lines with a straight ruler and rotary cutter.

4. Transfer the embroidery design over a lightbox to the centre of each of the quilter's muslin hexagons with a fine pencil or non-permanent marker. (You do not need to reverse the pattern.)

5. Iron the 8½″ pellon hexagon to the back of the 23 x 8 ½″ hexagons.

6. Embroider the muslin hexagons using your favourite stitches. I've used two strands of thread for chain stitch, stem stitch and the French knots on Peter Rabbit's tail. One strand of thread was used for the back stitch and the eyes are done in a fine satin stitch also using one strand of thread. See stitch guide in **General Instructions**

(page 9). Also take note of close up photos where I have added extra embroidered detail, e.g., the fence in the small Peter Rabbit.

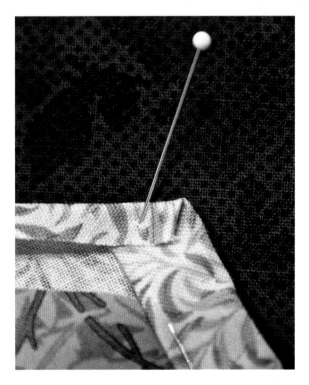

7. Each 10½″ hexagon back is now stitched to the 8½″ hexagon fronts. Centre each small hexagon over the larger one leaving a 1″ seam allowance round the edges–this allows for folds over the smaller hexagon.

8. Follow the step by step photos for the method of folding over each edge and pin in place.

9. Hand stitch folds in place using a small blind hem stitch as you would for a binding.

10. Prepare the four half hexagons for the top and bottom rows. Repeat as for full hexagons. (Note I did not do side set in hexagons.)

11. The folding of the edges is a little more tricky so follow the step by step photos. On each corner fold over once and then fold two "half folds" as shown.

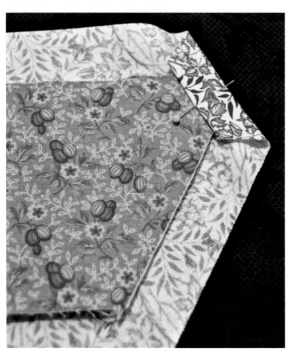

12. Handstitch folds down as before using a blind hem stitch and closing those mitred corners.

13. When all 23 hexagons and four half hexagons are completed lay them out in a pleasing order and pin numbers to assist with position while assembling.

14. Assembly: Starting with the top left hexagon and working across, join the hexagons by hand using a very tiny whip stitch. I did this from the back as you would for hand piecing tiny English paper pieced hexagons.

15. The final stitching I did was to hand quilt just inside each hexagon using a No. 12 Egyptian cotton from Wonderfil threads called Spagetti. It is a beautiful thread to work with as it is lint free and leaves the look of perle cotton.

Floral Frieze - Wall-Hanging

Beatrix demonstrated a natural talent for drawing at a very young age. Her father was a great friend of the Pre-Raphaelite artist John Everett Millais. One of Millais's paintings, *Ophelia*, became a firm favourite of hers and she stated it was *"probably one of the most marvellous pictures in the world."* I was so amazed at this connection in Beatrix's life as William Morris was a distant part of this Pre-Raphaelite group. As a child Beatrix's family would regularly holiday in Scotland staying at Dalguise House, Dunkeld. It was here at the age of 15 that Beatrix sketched an image of the plaster relief work frieze on the wall and it is this drawing that has inspired my small wall-hanging which has inevitably become very "Morris like"!

You will need:

- Background cream fabric 50 cm × 110 cm (20″ × 43″) (This is enough for the front and back with some left for hanging sleeves)

- 20 cm (8″) x width of fabric for binding

- Small scraps of fabric for appliqué (two greens, burgundy, blue, two purples and a yellow)

- Matching threads for appliqué (Stranded cottons for hand appliqué or machine embroidery threads for machine)

- Cream thread for quilting

- Fusible appliqué paper

- 25 cm × 70 cm (10″ × 28″) batting

- Optional brass bell pull set for hanging quilt

Method:

1. From the cream background fabric cut two rectangles 7½″ × 24 ½″. Put one aside for the backing.

2. Following the **General Instructions** (page 9) appliqué the "Floral Frieze" pattern once as shown and then once more but tracing on the reverse side of the pattern over a lightbox–one section is a mirror image of the other. Appliqué both sections to one cream rectangle.

> **TIP!**
>
> **Instead of tracing and cutting out seven little circles for the small purple flowers you can trace them whole like I have. When the flower is appliquéd you will not even know! I did the same for the burgundy sunflower shape too–so much quicker!**

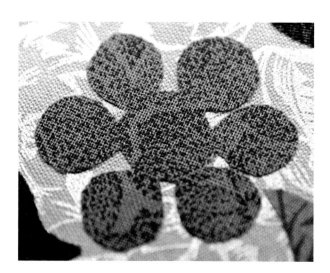

3. Sandwich the batting between the two cream rectangles, ensuring the right sides are facing outwards. Baste as desired–either pin or tack. My preference was to free motion quilt in a cream thread around the outside edge of the entire appliqué first. To do this you need to drop your feed-dogs on the machine and then use a free-motion quilting foot. I then echoed around the appliqué in a little tear drop shape and then finally a half feather design around the entire outside edge towards the appliqué.

4. Following the Binding section of the **General Instructions** (page 9), join on the cross, two 2½″ binding strips to make one long length. Press the strip in half, wrong sides together and raw edges even. Attach to the front of the quilt using a ¼″ seam and mitering the corners as you come to them. Trim back any excess batting and fold binding to the back of the quilt and hand stitch in place.

5. Finally, add hanging pockets and rods of your choice.

Daily Walk

Castle Cottage

The Tailor of Gloucester

Cherry Twist Cushion

I have thoroughly enjoyed re-reading some of Beatrix Potter's tales, especially the *Tailor of Gloucester*. It tells the story of a tailor who began to make a coat for the Mayor of Gloucester, who was to be married on Christmas day. The coat was made of "*cherry-coloured corded silk embroidered with pansies and roses*" with "*a waistcoat worked with poppies and corn-flowers.*" We soon learn that the tailor runs out of cherry twist and that he becomes very unwell and unable to complete the coat. While ill with fever the tailor mumbles "*no more twist, no more twist*" but some very clever little mice complete the outfit while he sleeps. They are unable to complete one buttonhole and leave a little note pinned to the waistcoat with the words "*no more twist.*" If you have a copy of this little tale do check Beatrix's beautiful art work of the embroidered waistcoat as this is where my cushion design comes from!

finished size 13″ × 20″ (33 cm × 50 cm)

You will need:

- Cream centre fabric 25 cm × 40 cm (10″ × 16″)
- Cherry coloured floral print 70 cm x width of fabric (43″/110 cm) (This is enough for the two panels either side of the cream centre and for the cushion back)
- Plain cherry coloured fabric for binding 20 cm (8″) x width of fabric (43″/110 cm)

- Assorted fabrics for appliqué (two greens, two blues, two cherry colours)
- Matching threads for appliqué and embroidery (Stranded cottons for hand appliqué or machine embroidery threads for machine)
- Matching thread for quilting and piecing
- Fusible appliqué paper

. . .You will need:

- 14″ × 21″ piece of batting to quilt cushion top
- 14″ (35 cm) dress zipper
- 80 cm cherry coloured ¼″ (5mm) ric rac
- Small pearl beads
- Approx 14″ × 21″ (35 cm × 55 cm) cushion insert (I like mine a little larger than the finished cushion so it is firmly stuffed)

Method:

1. From the cream centre fabric cut one rectangle 8½″ × 13½″.

2. From the cherry floral print cut two front side strips 6½″ × 13½″.

3. From the cherry floral print cut two pieces, 11½″ × 13½″ for backing.

4. Following the **General Instructions** (page 9) appliqué all pattern pieces to the cream centre. Take note that the flower stem and top of flower are embroidered. Use a chain stitch for the stem and French knots for the top of the flower.

5. Using a ¼″ seam attach the two side floral pieces to the completed centre. Your piece should now measure 13½″ × 20½″.

6. I've quilted my cushion top in a 1″ cross hatch grid. If you would like to do this just place the batting underneath, pin baste and quilt through all layers avoiding the appliqué.

7. I've attached a ¼″ cherry coloured ric rac using a straight stitch on the machine about ½″ in from the seam. I added the pearl beads inside each ric rac curve by hand.

8. Using one of the backing pieces of fabric turn under twice along the 13½″ length using a ½″ seam allowance for each fold. Machine baste seam down. Repeat for the other backing piece.

9. Pin the upper side of one zip edge to the under side of one of the folded and basted backing fabric pieces and using a zipper foot attach by machine. Note the zip is longer than required–this will make sense in the following steps.

12. Cut two strips of binding fabric 2½″ wide by length of fabric. Join to make one long piece of binding.

13. Pin layers together as you would a quilt and finally attach the 2½″ binding.

10. Repeat for the other side but overlapping the top to hide the zip.

14. Take care when stitching over zip ends. When folded over, the zip end looks very neat.

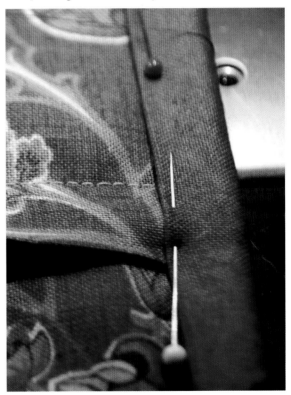

11. Move the zipper pull to the centre of the cushion and pin both ends and machine stitch to secure as seen in photo.

15. Finally insert cushion insert and enjoy.

THE PITKIN GUIDE TO

BEATRIX POTTER

PETER RABBIT

Beatrix Potter

BEATRIX POTTER
AND
PETER RABBIT

T
JEMI

T
M

Hill Top Wool Felt Storage Box

Beatrix Potter purchased Hill Top in 1905, perhaps with the plan for it to be her new home with the love of her life (and editor), Norman Warne. They dreamed of owning a farm in the Lakes district but sadly it was not to be as Norman died from leukaemia only a month after proposing. Filled with grief, Beatrix moved to Hill Top and for the next eight years she completed 13 stories. In 1909 Beatrix purchased a further property just over the road, Castle Cottage. It was in 1913 that Beatrix married Lakes district solicitor William Heelis. They lived together at Castle Cottage for 30 years. Beatrix kept Hill Top as a working farm but also a retreat where she could be creative with her drawing and writing. This wool felt storage box is my naïve version of Beatrix's beloved Hill Top.

You will need:

- Black wool felt piece 100 cm × 40 cm (40″ × 16″) for inner lining and outer box
- 20 cm × 20 cm (8″ × 8″) beige felt piece for main house (double this amount if appliquéing house to both sides of box)
- Small pieces of wool felt for windows, doors, porch roof, sheep and tree
- Stranded cottons or perle cotton threads for appliqué and embroidery

- Crewel needle for embroidery and chenille needle for assembling box
- Template plastic two pieces 13 cm × 13 cm (5″ × 5″) (for ends) and three pieces 13 cm × 23 cm (5″ × 9″) (front, back and base)
- Freezer paper—30 cm × 30 cm (12″ × 12″)
- Optional Handles (I purchased mine from Studio Mio: *www.studiomio.com.au*)

Method:

1. From the black wool felt cut three rectangles 5¾″ × 9¾″ and two squares 5¾″ × 5¾″. Repeat for the inner lining pieces.

2. Trace appliqué shapes from pattern sheet on to the paper side of the freezer paper. Cut out shape and iron the shiny side to the small pieces of wool felt for appliqué. Cut around the paper template. You can re-use the freezer paper a few times but peel off gently. You may prefer to pin the templates with tiny pins and cut around the edge. Be careful to tuck the centre chimney under the roof before stitching.

3. Embellish the house as your heart desires! I embellished mine with wisteria and a climbing rose. I used a stem stitch for the trunk and branches and purple French knots for wisteria, with a shade of deep pink for the climbing rose.

4. Attach the windows with a single strand of thread and long straight stitches from side to side.

5. When all appliqué is complete the sections are assembled. Take a lining rectangle and an outer rectangle, and with right sides together and using a ¼″ seam, machine stitch three sides together–leave one of the short sides open to insert template plastic. Repeat for the other three rectangles and the two end squares.

   Note: I have allowed a little extra seam allowance to accommodate the bulk of the folded wool felt inside the seam–hence template is 5″ × 5″ but wool felt squares were cut 5¾″ × 5¾″ as were the rectangles 5¾″ × 9¾″. I just found mine a little tight so have made adjustments accordingly.

6. Trim corners, turn right side out and insert template plastic.

7. Repeat this for all sections–two sides, one base and two ends. Pin and close the openings by hand with an overcast stitch.

8. Place each section on the table as shown in the photo and attach the sides and ends to each side of the base. With a chenille needle and matching perle cotton I used an overcast stitch (whip stitch) so it could not be seen.

Hilltop House by Karen de la Pena, Ventura, California
Private Collection

9. Finally hand stitch optional handles either end if desired.
   Enjoy your little box!

1863 – A Wedding Quilt

When I finally committed to writing this book, Helen suggested I might like to reproduce the quilt from Hill Top and make it a project for the book. I had seen a very simple patchwork quilt on the Hill Top website which I knew would be quite easy to reproduce. But when the images finally came through from the National Trust my jaw hit the floor! I knew I would not have the time (or patience) to piece all the blocks, so in my style of quilt making I decided to do the entire quilt in appliqué. Historically this quilt is of great significance and it only comes out for viewing on special occasions if requested–so I am honoured that I have been allowed to share all of this with you. It is thought that it may have been a wedding gift to Beatrix's parents and as her mother Helen Leech was a needlewoman, she may have contributed to the making of it. The centre panel reflects the wedding date and the initials of Rupert Potter and Helen Leech. The appliqué is, I think, quite whimsical, and records I have found state that the diamond shaped blocks are actually appliquéd to the quilt. On careful examination you will see nothing lines up and hexagons are cut to fit – works for me!

You will need:

All the requirements below are based on a width of fabric being 110 cm (43″) unless otherwise noted. Where a plain fabric was required I used some of the Modern Solid Collection from *In the Beginning Fabrics*. They are not traditionally dyed fabrics but woven dyed thread, resulting in the back and the front of the fabrics being identical and having a slight texture. The fabrics also have a high thread count so beautiful for appliqué.

- Background Centre: cream 2.6 metres (103″) (I used quilters' muslin)

- Hexagon border: black tone on tone print: 1.3 metres (51″)

- Outer border: 2.1 metres (8″) I used a print covered in very fine calligraphy to give an aged look and to acknowledge "Beatrix the writer"

- 20 Star blocks set on the centre diamond: In total you need 70 cm for base of star block (28″), 45 cm for stars (18″) and 60 cm (23″) for the strips around the block edge (If using an assortment of fabrics you need to allow a 6½″ square for each star base, 5½″ for each star and 1½″ × 25″ for the strips that surround the star. In total there are 20 star blocks)

- 44 Hexagon rosette blocks: In total you will need 107 cm (42″) for hexagon bases and 20 cm (8″) for centres (Allow 6″ × 6″ for each hexagon and 2½″ for each centre)

- 24 Kaleidoscope blocks (outer border): In total you will need 70 cm (27″) for base, 70 cm (26″) for contrast shape inside and 10 cm strip (4″) for black centres (Allow 8½″ each base and 8½″ each contrast shape inside)

- Black lozenge shapes in diamond surrounding star blocks: 90 cm (36″)

- Black lozenge shapes in outer border between kaleidoscope blocks: 70 cm (27″)

- Appliqué: 25 cm (10″) each of 2–3 greens, 20 cm (8″) each of purple, orange and burgundy for flowers, small scraps of brown and copper for acorns, 25 cm (10″) black for 16 four petal shapes inside large cream triangles

- 8 metres (8¾ yards) × 2.5 cm (1″) wide black ric rac

- At least 5 metres (5½ yards) of fusible appliqué paper (you need lots!)

- Black cotton for appliqué–the entire quilt was appliquéd in black only

- Cream and black cotton for quilting

- Binding: 60 cm × 110 cm (23½″ × 43″)

- Backing fabric: 5.2m × 110 cm (5¾ yards × 43″)

- Batting: 218 cm × 260 cm (86″ × 102″)

- Several sheets of template plastic to make block and appliqué templates

Now if you've got through that exhausting requirement list you might be overwhelmed–yes, it does use an awful lot of fabric and possibly you would need less if you pieced some of the blocks. But you will still need to appliqué the pieced blocks to each row. And you will find a design wall (or the floor in my case!) will be of great benefit when assembling the sections.

Original 1863 quilt, © National Trust

Method:

1. Prepare the large cream centre: You will need to join two strips to make a centre 49″ × 66″ (48½″ × 65½″ finished). I did this by cutting two strips 49″ x width of fabric and then joined them along the 49″ length. I then re-cut to get the final measurement–your seam will be horizontal in the centre of your quilt and once appliquéd you will not notice the seam.

2. Appliqué Centre: Fold the centre in half lengthways and widthways to find the centre and to assist with placement. Mark the centre with an X using a non-permanent marker. The outer oak leaf and acorn design are appliquéd either side of a circle approximately 15½″ in diameter. To make this circle, mark dots 7¾″ out from the centre several times and then join the dots. Following the **General Instructions** (page 9) and using the photo as a guide, appliqué the small leaves, oak leaves, berries and acorns.

3. When the acorn wreath is complete you can appliqué the leaves, flowers and berries in the centre. Use the pattern (pullout page P2) as a guide but remember this has been reversed for appliqué so you will need to place the wrong side of the pattern page under your background centre for correct placement.

4. When the centre appliqué is complete cut five 6½″ black hexagon border strips. Join two strips for each vertical border. Cut one strip in half and stitch each half to the two remaining strips–these are for the top and bottom borders. Measure through the centre of your quilt vertically before adding the side borders and horizontally before adding the top and bottom borders. You should need two vertical borders 6½″ × 66″ and two horizontal borders 6½″ × 61½″.

5. You are now ready to prepare the star blocks, lozenge shapes and hexagons for appliqué. *Note: you may like to just leave a narrow strip of fusible appliqué webbing on some of the larger blocks to reduce some of the layers. Trim out some of the fusible appliqué paper from the centers on larger shapes leaving a narrow margin along the edge before ironing to the wrong side of fabric–this is called windowing.*

> **Note:**
> **After I had completed the entire quilt I hand stitched (in chain stitch) the marked circle lines and tendrils as indicated on the pattern page. This includes the extra stems at the top and bottom of the design. I chose to do this at the end as you can embed the knot in the batting and I also like my stitches to sit on top of my work.**

6. Hexagon rosettes: I made templates for all pieces and found this easier to trace around on the fusible appliqué paper. Make a template and trace 44 large hexagon shapes and 44 centre hexagons to the paper side of the fusible appliqué paper. Cut just outside the line and then iron to the back of an assortment of fabrics. Once applied to fabric cut on the traced line. Before peeling off the backing fabric, place the small cream hexagon in the centre of each large rosette.

I found drawing pencil lines as indicated on the pattern (pullout page P1) most useful for both placement of this centre and also for blanket stitch guidance. I stitched around every shape to give the illusion of each hexagon being individually cut and appliquéd, but left the outer edge for appliquéing to the quilt background.

7. Star blocks: Each block (which is in fact an 8½″ hexagon), needs one base, one star and six strips around the edge. Repeat making templates and follow steps as before. You do not need to tuck under any pieces as you will stitch around every piece–the black stitching gives it the definition I was wanting. Using a blanket stitch, appliqué the entire centre of each block, leaving the outside edge to appliqué to the background.

8. Black lozenge shapes: Make templates as directed on the pattern (pullout page P2), including the leaves and round berry flower shapes. Follow as before and stitch with blanket stitch all areas except the outer edge.

9. You will need a design wall or floor for this stage. I think it is easier to lay it all on a blanket on the floor where you can press it all down. Lay out your prepared cream centre with black border, and using the photo as a guide, start placing the star block hexagon shapes. It will take time to get the diamond shape so be patient! You will notice that the top and bottom shapes lay over the black border and the inner upper and lower shapes overlap a little. The other lozenges fit in around the edges. There are different lozenge shapes on each corner as indicated on the pattern (pullout page P2). Play around and when you are happy press it all in place.

You will see in the above photo that the wreath has not been applied. I wished I had done the wreath first. The instructions now reflect that.

10. Take the quilt top to the machine and blanket stitch the outside edges of each appliqué piece. *I fold the quilt into sections and safety pin the area I am not appliquéing–this helps prevent areas from lifting and fraying.* Place the four petal flowers (16 in total, 4 in each corner) in place and appliqué them as well. Take note of position with the quilt photo on page 50. Note that the black ric rac is the very last thing to be applied (*after* quilting).

11. Kaleidoscope blocks: Prepare templates as before. This is where you might really want to use the windowing of the fusible paper (cutting a "window" of excess fusible appliqué paper), before you iron to the large base shape. This block is really just an 8″ × 8″ square with the four wedge shapes ironed to the top and then the corners are trimmed (see pullout page P1). You will need to make 24 large blocks and two smaller blocks in total.

12. Blanket stitch the wedge shape and centre circle to the base of each block, leaving the outside edge for later.

13. Prepare outer borders: Cut nine strips x 9″ across the width of the fabric. Cut one strip in half and set aside. Join two full width strips together and attach one of the half strips set aside. Repeat this for the two vertical side borders. Your vertical side borders should need to be 78″ but measure through the centre of your quilt lengthways to check your own measurement. (Do not apply to the quilt yet.) With the four strips left, join two together and repeat so you have two strips joined for the horizontal top and bottom border. Your horizontal borders should also need to be 78″ (strange coincidence!), but again check by measuring through the centre of your quilt widthways and cut to size before applying.

14. Press appliqué pieces to outer borders. This is where you will need to do some fudging as I did to make it all fit. Some of the black lozenges need trimming (they will need to be slightly narrower than 4″ wide to fit), and you will notice that if you look closely! I also needed to apply a smaller kaleidoscope block in the centre of the top and bottom horizontal borders so take note of that. I don't feel so bad as it was indeed challenging designing the entire quilt from a small photo, and of course looking at the original there was a huge amount of fudging that occurred–I wonder what quilters called it back in 1863?!

15. Take borders to the machine and blanket stitch around the outside edges before attaching to the quilt. I rolled the excess border and placed it in a plastic bag so that the only section I was appliquéing was exposed. This keeps the rest of your work out of the way while stitching, preventing the appliqué from lifting or the border edges fraying.

16. Backing: Cut the length of backing fabric in half making two pieces approximately 218 cm wide by 260 cm long (86″ × 102″). (Batting needs to be same size.)

17. Quilting: Sandwich quilt top, batting and backing, and pin or hand baste layers together. Attach the walking foot or engage the dual feed and stitch in the ditch around each border. Remove the walking foot and replace with a free motion quilting foot. Machine quilt around each block following the centre line of blanket stitch and as shown on pattern (pullout page P1) for each section. For the hexagons I followed the centre of the blanket stitch, and for the star hexagons I quilted leaf shapes in the centre of each piece and straight lines in the outer border blocks. I also machine quilted veins in the centre wreath leaves in a contrasting dark thread. The background was quilted with tear drop shapes and feathers.

18. Following the Binding section of the **General Instructions** (page 9) join on the cross, nine 2½″ binding strips to make one long length. Press the strip in half, wrong sides together and raw edges even. Attach to the front of the quilt using a ¼″ seam and mitering the corners as you come to them. Trim back any excess batting and fold binding to the back of the quilt and hand stitch in place.

19. The final step in my quilt was the hand embroidery. As stated in step two, I hand-stitched the drawn 15½″ circle between the appliquéd oak leaves, small leaves, berries and acorns. I finally added tendrils as indicated on pattern. I like to do this final step when the quilt is quilted and bound, as I can embed the knot in the batting and allow my stitches to sit on the surface.

Michele Hill
www.michelehillquilts.com
williammorrisandmichele.blogspot.com.au

Further Reading and Bibliography

Beatrix Potter –
The Extraordinary life of a Victorian Genius
Linda Lear, 2008 (Penguin)

The Tale of Peter Rabbit, 1902

The Tailor of Gloucester, 1903

The Tale of Squirrel Nutkin, 1903

The Tale of Two Bad Mice, 1904

The Tale of Benjamin Bunny, 1904

The Tale of Mrs Tiggy-Winkle, 1905

The Tale of Jeremy Fisher, 1906

The Tale of Jemima-Puddle-Duck, 1908

The Tale of Mrs Tittlemouse, 1910

Beatrix Potter (Frederick Warne/Penguin)

Serendipity

Some of you may have seen me hand embroidering these blocks on my blog and luck would have it that we have room in the book to share my progress! By the time the book is printed the quilt should be well and truly finished and I will ensure there are photos on my blog for you to see.

While thinking of a name for my partially completed quilt I came up with *Serendipity* and immediately did a search to check it was the right word. I loved that the first meaning I found was "a pleasant surprise," so I hope this truly is a pleasant surprise to you as it was to me when I was told that I needed to fill up a few more pages before going to print! I was also intrigued that it was a Horace Walpole who used the word in a letter in 1754 to a colleague where he shared a book that he was reading, a Persian fairy tale *The Three Princes of Serendip*. He explained in the letter that the princes were always making discoveries quite by accident–so the word *serendipity* came into being. I am glad that this serendipitous moment came about and that you could see this "bonus project" even unfinished! This also highlights how any of the supplied designs in the book can be used in different ways. Many of these blocks can be seen in the *Bubbles* quilt on page 23, but here I have hand embroidered them instead of appliquéing.

You will need:

- Background fabric for nine square blocks (pale grey spot in my quilt) 110 cm metres x width of fabric (110 cm) (43" × 43")
- Pale blue print for 'petals' surrounding the embroidered circles 50 cm x width of fabric (110 cm) (20" × 43")
- White tone on tone print for the nine circles that will be embroidered 100 cm x width of fabric (110 cm) (39" × 43")
- White fabric for the back of the nine circles: 100 cm x width of fabric (110 cm) (39" × 43")
- Iron on stabiliser (weaveline, whisperweft or similar) to back the nine circles that will be embroidered: 100 cm x width of fabric (110 cm) (39" × 43")

- Blue print for sashings, outer border and binding 1.8 m x width of fabric (110 cm) (70" × 43")
- Backing fabric needs to measure 60" × 60" (155 cm × 155 cm)
- Batting needs to measure 60" × 60" (155 cm × 155 cm)
- Grey or beige thread (a neutral colour) for piecing and matching background thread to quilt
- Fusible applique paper
- An assortment of stranded cottons for embroidery. I used several variegated shades from Cottage Garden threads as I did in the Handmade Hexie project
- Piece of template plastic to make the petal shape – 20 cm × 10 cm (8" × 4")

Cutting:

1. From the background fabric cut three 13½" strips across the width of fabric and then crosscut to yield nine 13½" × 13½" squares. These will be your nine background blocks ready for the circles and petals to be appliquéd after the designs have been embroidered. Set aside for later.

2. From the white tone on tone fabric cut three 12" strips across the width of fabric and then crosscut to yield nine 12" × 12" squares.

3. From the stabiliser cut nine 12" × 12" squares to back the white tone on tone print blocks in preparation for embroidery. My preference is weaveline that has a fine organza texture that can be ironed to the back of the fabric. Having a stabiliser helps the stitches to sit nicely and gives a great base if working in an embroidery hoop. *Note: the circles are cut after the embroidery is complete.*

4. From the white backing fabric cut nine x 9" circles-this includes a ¼" seam allowance so that the completed circles are 8½" finished. These will be stitched to the back of the completed embroideries. Put aside.

5. From the blue sashing fabric you will need six strips 2½" × 13½" to join blocks vertically into rows and a further two strips 2½" × 43½" for the two horizontal rows.

6. From the remainder of the sashing fabric the outer borders are cut 6½" wide-six strips in total (1 and a bit for each side) and the binding 2½" wide-six strips also required.

7. The blue petal fabric does not need to be cut-this is for appliqué only.

Method:

1. Transfer the embroidery designs over a lightbox to the centre of each of the white tone on tone squares with a fine pencil or non-permanent marker.

2. Embroider each design using stitches of choice as seen in the Handmade Hexie project. I have gained more confidence since making the Hexie quilt and added a little more texture like the lazy daisies and French knots in Jemima's cape!

3. When all nine blocks are embroidered fold the blocks in half lengthways and widthways and finger press to find the centre. Mark with a pin. Using a compass or template and ensuring the design is centred mark a 9″ circle from the centre out (using a fine pencil or non-permanent marker). When you are happy with placement cut on the pencil line.

4. Using a ¼″ seam allowance and with right sides together stitch the 9″ white backing circles to the completed embroidered circles.

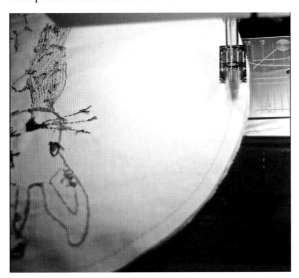

5. Taking note of the photo carefully make a slit in each backing circle and turn right side out. A chopstick helps to ease out the seam. Press firmly and set aside.

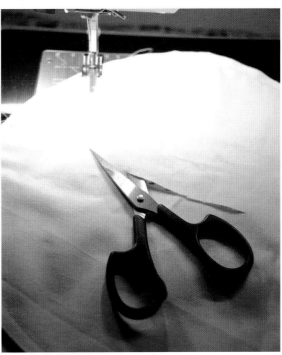

6. Prepare the petal template as provided using template plastic. I found this was the most economical way of using fabric-complete petal circles would have needed a lot more!

7. Following the **General Instructions** (page 9) trace four petal shapes for each block-you will need 36 shapes in total-four around each circle. Cut out and set aside.

8. Fold the grey background blocks in half lengthways and widthways and finger press to find the centre. Repeat this with the completed embroidered circles and pin to the centre of the background block. Tuck under the petal shapes lining up with the folded lengthways and widthways lines. You could mark these and place the petals in place before adding the circle but I would not press into place until you are sure the circle covers the raw edge curves. I preferred to centre the circle and then tuck the petal shapes underneath the circle.

9. Appliqué all pieces to the background. Note in the photo where I have stitched all the way to the edge of the circle giving the illusion of separate petals.

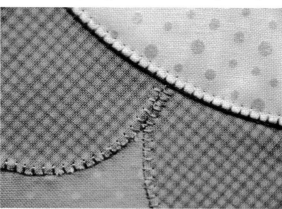

10. Join the blocks to the 2½″ sashing strips as shown in the diagram for the *Bubbles* quilt project. Continue with the vertical sashing strips again following the *Bubbles* quilt project.

11. The final construction of the quilt is to attach the 6½″ borders.

12. When the quilt top is completed prepare backing fabric to measure approx. 60″ × 60″.

13. Continue to follow the steps in the *Bubbles* project and quilt as desired. I am not quite sure how I will do that yet!

¼ of design

I hope you enjoy stitching your own special creations with all the designs from the pattern pages in this book and I would love to see photos of your finished work too please!

And one final note from me – all the pattern pages in the book have a very fine perforation so carefully remove each one and store in a plastic sleeve for future use. Enjoy x

Beloved View by Jennifer Johnson, Private Collection
Beatrix Potter's view from her window before she died